The School Essay Manifesto

The School Essay Manifesto

Reclaiming the Essay for Students and Teachers

Thomas Newkirk

Foreword by Barry Lane

Discover Writing Press

Discover Writing Press

P. O. Box 264
Shoreham, Vermont 05770
800-613-8055
www.discoverwriting.com

ISBN 1-931492-17-4

Library of Congress Control Number: 2005931953

Design by Bookwrights Design

05 06 07 08 09 10 11   10 9 8 7 6 5 4 3 2

First Edition

For information on workshops, professional development and lesson plans, please visit our website at:

For Donald Murray

Contents

Foreword

Mr. Socrates and Mr. Newkirk Meet Mr. Writing Textbook

My wife and I have a passion for listening to college courses on tape. There is something enthralling about sitting in traffic while pondering great philosophical ideas and in the back of your mind knowing there will be no mid-term test to study for. Recently, I started a course entitled "American Civilization." The professor began with a discussion of the prerequisite conditions for each form of government as noted by Montesquieu in his essay, "Spirit of the Laws." Dictatorships, according to Montesquieu, required a fearful public; feudal societies depended upon a noble ruling class; but democracy was different. Democracy depended on the virtue of each citizen.

Virtue. The word itself has an ancient ring to it. I was drawn back to my philosophy class, freshman year of college, 1974. That was the first time I read the words of Socrates in Plato's dialogue, "The Euthyphro." Socrates argues for the existence of virtue (arête) among human beings, not just blind obedience to the gods practiced by the masses of the time. I remember being impressed by Socrates's style of arguing. He did not coerce; he did not bully; but, with simple questions, he gained a foothold into Euthyphro's unquestioning mind and slowly helped lead him to the truth.

Fast forward 10 years to 1983, graduate school, University of New Hampshire. I sit in the "Teaching Writing Methods" class of Thomas Newkirk. He has asked us to read Plato's dialogue, "Phaedrus," and reflect on Socrates's disdain for writing, the new information storage technology of the day. Socrates worries that writing will inhibit the free flow of ideas that arise from conversation. Writing will formalize half-baked

truths. At first, I think it odd that the first reading assignment in a class about teaching writing
should be an attack on writing itself from no less
an authority than the great Socrates. But then
again, this is not a normal class and Newkirk is
not your typical professor. He does not lecture to
us from a podium but sits with us in a circle and
conducts what is more of a class conversation
than a class discussion. He does not wear the
classic tweed sport coat but dons V-neck sweat-
ers with sleeves rolled up to the elbows. Most revealing of all, he doesn't come to class with tidy
lessons in a proper briefcase, rather, he ambles
into the room with armloads of student papers,
dog-eared novels, and scholarly books. He pres-
ents his lessons as experiments that he tries out
on us and then asks us to draw conclusions. He
seems surprised and delighted by our interpretations; he questions our assumptions then adds
his own opinions and scholarship. He insists we
call him Tom, and it is soon apparent to everyone
in the class that Tom is not here to teach us. Like
Socrates, Tom is here to open our minds.

As you prepare to read The School Essay
Manifesto, get ready to have your mind opened.
Thomas Newkirk has written a book that will
revolutionize the way you think about essays

and may even change the way you teach essay writing. Newkirk's basic hypothesis is that the school essay as we know it is an obsolete assignment that evolved out of the need for teachers and textbook companies to control student writing, organize student's thoughts and more easily grade writing assignments. Real essay writers, such as EB White or Michel de Montaigne (the historical father of the essay), knew that the essay was a playful, free flowing form and more a way of exploring your thoughts on a subject than proving a thesis statement. Newkirk traces the origins of the thesis-control essay, shows examples of student essays that break the mold and suggests assignments to liberate student writing from the textbook forms that ensnare it.

Not every English teacher will agree with Newkirk's thesis. After all, isn't the job of English teachers to give students basic forms and structures like the 5 paragraph theme or "the hamburger paragraph" (topic sentence, 3 supporting details, conclusion). If you want to be Chopin, don't you first have to start by learning a few scales on the piano? This may all be true, but, then again, isn't there more to writing than just filling out forms? Isn't there a higher cognitive purpose in writing an essay—a quest for truth, perhaps, a striving for virtue? Does not a democracy depend on this striving? What will become of our American Democracy if our citizens' writings are only the means of backing up their previously held opinions and not seen as a means for discovering objective reality or staking out the common ground which unites us? Won't we become a land divided into camps, a land of fixed conclusions, a land controlled by sound bytes and emotional manipulation, where demagogues can define truth for their own corrupt purpose and be assured that no one but the opposition party will question them? When people stop thinking, when people stop questioning, when people stop looking for truth, can we even still call it a democracy?

Ask Mr. Socrates, or ask Mr. Newkirk. You'll find them in the marketplace corrupting the youth.

Barry Lane
Shoreham, VT

Introduction

Near the end of *Catcher in the Rye*, Holden Caulfield describes an "Oral Expression" class at one of the many prep schools he has attended. Students in the class were instructed to yell "digression" whenever anyone went off the subject. One student, Richard Kinsella, was a special target because in a speech on his farm in Vermont he didn't stick to describing the animals, vegetables, "and stuff" that grew on the farm:

> What he did was, Richard Kinsella, he'd *start* telling you all about that stuff—then all of a sudden he'd start telling you about this letter his mother got from his uncle, and how his uncle got polio when he was forty-two years old, and how he didn't want anybody to see him with a brace on.

> It didn't have much to do with the farm—I
> admit it—but it was *nice*.... I mean it's dirty
> to keep yelling "Digression!" at him when
> he's all nice and excited.

Holden, it seems to me, is endorsing a theory of language that acknowledges its suggestiveness, the way it can leap ahead of our intentions and plans—and in doing so we find even richer topics for expression. Donald Murray describes this process as "listening to the text," as taking guidance from the "informing line." William Stafford speaks of an attitude of receptivity. Holden's teacher, on the other hand, endorses a strict sense of "topic" that precludes these leaps and associations that are essential to essay writing as I describe it in this short manifesto.

My favorite example of this open stance to language is the 18th century novel, *The Life and Opinions of Tristram Shandy,* which opens with the moment of Tristram's conception (he blames his future psychological problems on the fact that the hall clock struck at the precise moment of insemination). The narrator then takes almost two hundred pages to get to his own birth. He is constantly sidetracked. For example, he begins to talk about a dispute between his mother and father, only to interrupt himself:

My mother, you must know,—but I have fifty things more necessary to let you know first,—I have a hundred difficulties which I have promised to clear up, and a thousand distresses and domestic adven-tures crouding in on me, thick and three-fold, one upon the neck of another... (174)

Tristram Shandy is a novel about the impossibility of writing a novel. It mocks straight-forwardness, coherence, the narrative line— "for if he is a man of the least spirit, he will have fifty deviations from a straight line to make with this or that party as he goes along, which he can no ways avoid."

One basic way to imagine this stance toward language is to imagine two types of meanings that words can hold. One is the more literal, sentence-specific sense of the word; the other is the wider set of connotations and associations that the word evokes for writer and reader. For example, I can write the sentence:

I grew up in Ashland, Ohio.

As it stands in the sentence, "Ashland" is a location in Ohio, little more. But as I write the word "Ashland," it leaps beyond the limits of the sentence and sets off a chain of impressions and memories. It is, in Vygotsky's terms, "saturated with sense." It reminds me, among other things, of the summer of 1969 when torrential rains caused the town creek to overflow and flood downtown businesses. The governor declared Ashland a "disaster area" drawing from my friend Tom McNaull the comment, "Well, it's about time." Which leads to another memory....

In this one, I am at the city pool where I worked during the summers. It was early evening, the pool lights had just been turned on, and two older lifeguards, Dick Lifer and Bob Doerrer, were discussing their plans for the night. Dick asked, "What time is it anyway?" The answer was 8:15. "Damn," he replied, "it never gets late in this town."

In conversation we are always alert to these triggering moments. We never worry about having enough to say when we are with friends. We assume that talk will lead to talk, story to story, joke to joke, language to language—even though we have nothing planned, always better if we have nothing planned.

I realize that writing is not simply structureless digression, that information needs shape, that even the most generous reader can be frustrated by Shandy's fifty deviations. Yet for inexperienced writers—which is to say almost all of the students we teach—the problems I see are more likely to be too much order, or rather a structure with not enough inside to need structuring. We have an enclosure but no wild animals to be controlled. While textbooks speak of theses and topic sentences as little generals controlling the unruly information, there is really precious little chaos to push back.

Montaigne, of course, is our great mentor in all this. Recently, I had a chance to see a facsimile of the 1588 quarto edition of his essays, upon which he made his final additions, expanding the essays by forty percent. On page after page he filled the huge margins with additions and commentaries, sometimes in the form of pasted slips of paper (latter day sticky notes). I could follow the way a word or name would trigger an anecdote or remind Montaigne of a new quotation. In the end, he saw the essays as almost infinitely expandable—"as long as there are ink and paper in the world."

I hope that this short monograph, miraculously reborn as a pocket-size manifesto, can assist teachers and students in embracing this chaotic, associative, generative stance toward language use. Because, as always, Holden is right. It *is* dirty to keep yelling "Digression!"

"If I had written to seek the world's favor, I should have bedecked myself better, and should present myself in a studied position. I want to be seen here in my simple, natural, ordinary, fashion, without straining for artifice; for it is myself I portray. My defects will here be read to the life, and also my natural form, as far as respect for the public has allowed. Had I been placed among those nations which are said to live still in the sweet freedom of nature's first laws, I assure you that I should have very gladly portrayed myself here entire and whole naked."

—Michel de Montaigne

in the introduction to his first book of essays (1580)

The School Essay (Bad Memories of)

In middle school, my daughter once complained about one of her writing assignments.

"Dad, I have to write an essay."

"Oh," I said, "what's so bad about that?"

She then assumed a stance that I'm convinced girls learn in sixth grade—one hand on the hip, head thrown back, eyes rolling. It's the stance that expresses a sixth grader's amazement at the ignorance of her parents. "It's so restricting. We have to have one main point which we state in the introduction. We have to have at least three examples or subpoints; we have to have a conclusion where we state our points in a more dramatic way. Oh, and we can't use *I*."

These guidelines are ones I've heard before, the ones that I had to follow in writing school essays over 20 years ago. And I remember feeling the same restriction. I remember wanting to respond with the schoolyard comeback, "Says who?" Who said an essay had to be this way? The answer, of course, was the writing textbooks we used, Lucile Vaughan Payne's *The Lively Art of Writing* and John Warriner's *English Grammar and Composition.*

Returning to these books, I found Payne's invitation to writers, encouraging us to think of ourselves as builders. Yet after the invitation, she presented us with the design for the building we were to construct (Figure 1).

According to Payne, the first paragraph begins broadly and narrows to a point; the middle section is the argument that takes up most of the essay; and the concluding paragraph begins at a narrow point and ends broadly.

Then, in italics, she claims that "this basic structure never changes." Her model would not constrict us though, because "just as different architects, beginning with the same design, willcreate completely different houses, so will the essayists

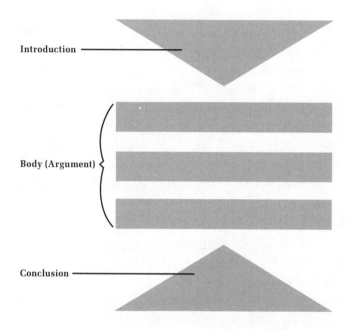

Figure 1. Structure of the Essay

create completely different essays (1965, p.48)." Even as an eager-to-please junior in high school, I realized that her advice was either meaningless (everything begins and ends) or it was unduly restrictive.

Payne also enjoined us from using "I"; in fact, it was one of her Two Commandments (the other was never to use "there"). She told us that we would weaken our writing if we said "I believe" or "I think." We were told that we could say, "God exists" but not "I believe that God exists." The first statement, according to Payne, had an "air of authority" (p. 71) that the second lacked. It is not clear how Payne would have students avoid the first person if they were using their own experiences as evidence for an opinion—something most easy writers do.

Throughout both *The Lively Art of Writing* and Warriner's *English Grammar and Composition* we were warned of the hazards of disorder. If we were constructing a building, we couldn't afford to omit a stairway or put the windows in unevenly. Writing was serious business that needed serious planning:

> Some people like to take aimless trips, making no plans at all but rambling over the countryside, exploring side roads, stopping when they wish, and not much caring when or where they arrive. When people want to reach a definite destination at a specific time, however, they generally make detailed plans of their route and

schedule their time.

Writing is much the same. Some writing—letters to friends, for example—is unplanned. It rambles on aimlessly and spontaneously, making digressions and having no fixed objective. For most formal writing, however, you need a plan which shows you where you are headed and how you expect to get there. (Warriner, Whitten, and Griffith, 1965, pp. 275-276).

Similarly, Payne told us that "the full thesis is your only sure guide through the tangle of ideas that always surround an essay topic." Of course, warnings like this were consistent with the moral training we were receiving in the mid-60s; we needed clear goals (a life-thesis, if you will) that would help us avoid the entanglements of alcohol, sex, and pleasure in general.

These textbooks betrayed themselves when they gave examples of the kind of writing we were to produce. Payne gave us this example of an effective opening paragraph:

The American buggy race is a thing of the past, but its spirit is not. Unfortunately, its spirit has undergone almost as complete a transformation as the racetrack and the

> vehicles themselves. The dirt track of the country fair has become a dragstrip, the buggy has become a hotrod, and the daring but friendly spirit of the contest has become a frightening and obsessive competition—often to the death (p. 51).

We knew this writing was false, skilled at a superficial level, but false. It was not rooted in conviction, in the experience of the writer, and would therefore not enter the experience of the reader. It was what Jerome Harste has called a "textoid," an artificial creation. It was not an essay.

The essay, I wanted to tell my daughter, was something different, something better, something looser, more personal, more playful. To understand an essayist, it may be necessary to watch a child with a rattle. Watch her shake it with one hand, then with two, watch her drop it, pick it up, hit it against the floor, and put it in her mouth. This is play, but as Piaget has shown, play central to the development of intelligence. The essayist also plays, though his play is internalized—looking at ideas from different directions, shaking them, pushing them until they fall over, pulling on them to look at their roots.

The essayist also believes that the reader is interested in this process of exploration. Edward Hoagland writes:

> A personal essay is like a human voice talking, its order the mind's natural flow, instead of a systematized outline of ideas. Though more wayward and informal than an article or treatise, somewhere it contains a point which is its real center, even if the point couldn't be uttered in fewer words than the essayist has used. Essays don't usually boil down to a summary, as articles do, and the style of the writer has a nap to it, a combination of personality and energetic loose ends that stands up like the loose nap on a piece of wool and can't be brushed flat (1985, p. 223).

In defining the essay, Hoagland also describes the act of critical thinking. We want students to make personal connections with ideas and texts, and we need forums, both oral and written, where these connections can be made. The essay can be one of these forums—if we will only reclaim it.

The Case Against Writing–Plato's Challenge

The case *for* writing is so widely accepted that it is difficult to imagine the case against it. Writing, we like to believe, makes us smarter, helps us think in new ways, makes us better citizens. Historians of literacy like Walter Ong (1977) and Jack Goody (1968, 1977) have claimed that alphabetic literacy virtually transformed the Western mind, allowing for a kind of analytic thought inaccessible to people from oral cultures. Educators like Janet Emig (1977) have claimed that writing is a unique mode of thinking because the writer can examine his or her own emerging text. She quotes the Russian psychologist A. R. Luria:

> (Written speech) assumes a much slower, repeated mediating process of analysis and synthesis, which makes it possible not only to develop the required thought, but even to revert to the earlier stages, thus transforming the sequential chain of connections in a simultaneous, self-reviewing structure (p. 128).

Writing, according to this view, allows both for thought to emerge and for the writer to transform the thought through self-review.

The air is so filled with claims like these that any counterclaims would seem both preposterous and anti-intellectual. Indeed, any argument to the contrary (if it is to go beyond the range of my voice) must—paradoxically—be written. Yet, Plato makes the apparently self-contradictory argument against literacy in his dialogue, *Phaedrus*. In the latter part of the dialogue, Plato's character, Socrates, begins to examine methods of teaching rhetoric and in this examination makes a celebrated and puzzling criticism of written language:

> ...writing involves a similar disadvantage to painting. The productions of painting look like live beings, but if

you ask them a question, they maintain a solemn silence. The same holds true for written words; you might suppose that they understand what they are saying, but if you ask them what they mean by anything they simply return the same answer over and over again (1973, p. 97).

Socrates claims that writing lacks the openness of conversation; writing is fixed where conversation can move *toward* wisdom. In conversation (even one with an uncritical admirer like young Phaedrus), positions can be developed, clarified, challenged—yet writing only gives the "same answer over and over again."

I suggest that we take this criticism seriously if we want to get beyond slogans linking writing and thinking. Do current approaches to teaching expository writing promote or do they actually foreclose possibilities for open-ended, conversation-like, exploration? Or does the "thesis-control essay" (the adult version of the "essay" my daughter was asked to write), the mainstay of expository writing programs, actually limit the inquiry that writing supposedly should foster? Is the level of "preformulation" needed to produce such an essay consistent with the view that writing can help the student explore a subject? And does this requirement to formulate a thesis and "defend" it bear any resemblance to what essay writers do?

The thesis-control essay, as it is taught in schools, is a simplified version of the classical argumentative form. And while we often ask students to support a position, we mean something very close to "defend." In fact, the classical rhetoricians viewed the speaker as participating in a contest or struggle where he (and it was, of course, a "he") must be able to fend off attacks. In making an assertion, the writer is staking out a territory that must be defended. To carry the imagery a bit further, if the speaker makes too bold or too broad an assertion—stakes out too much territory—the requirements for defense may be too great. The outer perimeter may be too porous. We see this imagery in the rituals of academic life, where doctoral students must defend their dissertations, presumably from the "attacks" of professors they have worked with for years. In this confrontative climate, indecision, confusion perplexity, contradiction, and even self-revelation may be interpreted as signs of weakness.

Janet Emig has referred to the thesis-control format as "the fifty star theme":

> A species of extensive writing that re-curs so frequently in student accounts that it deserves special mention is the *five-paragraph theme*, consisting of one para-graph of introduction ("tell what you are going to say"), three of expansion ("say it"), and one of conclusion ("tell what you have said"). This mode is so indig-enously American that it might be called the Fifty-star Theme. In fact, the reader might imagine behind this and the next three paragraphs Kate Smith singing "God Bless America" or the piccolo obligato from "Stars and Stripes Forever" (p.93).

This essay form has been variously depicted as a kind of hourglass (see Sheridan Baker's The Practical Stylist, 1986), as a hamburger, or, in a recent Sandra Boynton cartoon, as a dinosaur with a long, heavy, limp tail which "goes over ground that has already been covered."

My own doubts about the thesis-control essay crystallized during the year I directed a writing center at a large university. Most of the students who used the center came in for help on critical analysis papers, and many were non-native speakers who found the texts difficult to read in the first place. Yet the prescribed form allowed no room for the bafflement they were experiencing; their task on these papers was to assert and support—not to explore. They were to begin with conclusion, not questions. The confused students at the tutoring desk bore no resemblance to the quasi-assured persona needed for their papers. Presumably, though, they could use writing to find a way out of this confusion—to define, for example, what was puzzling them—but this step would not mesh with the form they were expected to use. David Bartholomae (1983) described this dilemma:

> When, for example, we ask students to write about texts, the tyranny of the thesis often invalidates the very act of analysis we hope to invoke. Hence, in assignment after assignment, we find students asked to reduce a novel, a poem, or their own experience into a single sentence, and then to use the act of writing in order to defend or "support" that single sentence. Writing is used to close a subject down rather than to open it up, to put an end to discourse rather than to open up a project. (p. 311).

The curious misdirection of the thesis-control essay is suggested by the clear requirement to students that the essay be used to "back up" the thesis. The reader is expected to move forward in a text that is continually backing up.

The problem with the thesis-control format is that it is not confined to the struggling students like those I saw in the writing center. The better student who masters this format may be at even more of a disadvantage because it becomes so easy to "slot in" evidence for the assertions in the opening paragraph. According to Russel Durst (1984), who conducted a case study of three high-achieving students and drawing on over 400 pieces of writing completed over a nine-year span, the thesis-control paper often becomes so formulaic that "these structures may have eventually limited the development of these writers" (p. 102).

James Marshall (1988) has shown how students plug into the thesis-control format in such a way that their writing is terrifyingly uniform. He quotes the openings from several student papers that dealt with the "code hero" in *The Sun Also Rises*, a topic discussed frequently in the class he studied. Here are two:

Ernest Hemingway, author of *The Sun Also Rises*, has very definite ideas as to what a man should be. The name given to this ideal is a "code hero." A code hero is brave, courageous, and independent. Many of Hemingway's novels contain a code hero. In *The Sun Also Rises*, Hemingway gives profiles of many men, four of them are Robert Cohn, Mike Campbell, Jake Barnes, and Pedro Romero.

In Ernest Hemingway's *The Sun Also Rises*, the men of the book have different personalities. Hemingway's novels sometimes share a type of man called the code hero who is Hemingway's idea of a true man. The code hero can drink without getting drunk, can have as many women as he wants, and most of all is brave. Robert Cohn, Mike Campbell, Jake Barnes, and Pedro Romero share some of these qualities that determine a "code hero."

We know what comes next—paragraphs on Cohn, Campbell, Barnes, and Romero. As one student put it, "It's automatic."

In the case of these Hemingway papers, the students are simply rehashing class notes. But even when students attempt to formulate their own theses, their results are often disappointing. Students are caught in a bind. On the one hand, they are asked to be provocative, to say something "interesting" about a text. And they are asked to make sure that every point they make is fully supported and that each relates to the major point stated in the first paragraph. They are to be adventurous but cautious; provocative but fully under control. Caught in this dilemma, the student often produces something like this opening paragraph:

> In the book, *I Know Why the Caged Bird Sings,* the theme of religion is found throughout the storyline. During the story, religion is also involved in Maya's life and brought to her through her grandmother, who she called "Mama" (Bean-Thompson, in press).

The next paragraph begins, as you might expect, "One example of religion...." This thesis is "defendable" but it is not "interesting." The writer can achieve certainty—but only by stressing the obvious. As teachers, we groan when we see students documenting the obvious. We wonder how this writer could be so sharp in class discussion and so dull in writing. But the writing is the perhaps inevitable result of the mixed messages we send.

Yet despite fairly persistent lampooning, the form is alive and well, dominating the expository writing class if not exactly flourishing there.

The reasons for its persistence are, I believe, bound up in deeply rooted notions about what the essay is. I suspect that many teachers teach the form—or variants of it—because they see no teachable alternative. The school essay has become the essay.

3

"For it is myself that I portray": Montaigne's Legacy

If the school essay is a watered-down version of academic disputation, the personal essay was created as a challenge to that scholastic tradition. And its originator is, of course, Michel de Montaigne. Even in his opening letter to his readers, Montaigne distances himself from serious discourse:

> Reader, lo here a well-meaning Book. It doth at the first entrance forewarn thee that in contriving the same I have proposed unto myself no other than a familiar and private aim.... Had my intention been to forestall and purchase the world's opinion and favor, I would surely have adorned

41

> myself more quaintly or kept a more solemn march (1959, p. xxiii).

There is an element of false modesty in this introduction. In fact, he was challenging the most basic beliefs of those who "kept a more solemn march"—the academic specialists of his day. He was challenging the belief that the world consisted of fixed entities that can be named and categorized with precision. And, as Spellmeyer (1989) has argued, he was challenging their belief in specialization, which separated the logician from the grammarian, and which separated the "high" language of the court and college from the "low" language of the street and home.

For Montaigne the act of knowing was, in reality, the art of wondering (Covino, 1988). The act of pursuing knowledge was the "proper business" of the man, but "to possess (knowledge) belongs to a higher power" (1580, 1959, p. 293). And in this pursuit, Montaigne acknowledges—even delights in—his own "unstable posture":

> Not only does the wind of accident move me at will, but besides, I am moved and disturbed as a result merely of my own unstable posture; and anyone who observes carefully can hardly find himself twice

in the same state. I give my soul now one
face, now another, according to which direction I turn it. If I speak of myself in different ways, that is because I look at myself
in different ways. All contradictions may
be found in me by some twist and in some
fashion. Bashful, insolent; chaste, lascivi-
ous; talkative, taciturn; tough, delicate;
clever, stupid; surly, affable; lying, truth-
ful; learned, ignorant; liberal, miserly, and
prodigal: all this I see in myself to some
extent according to how I turn; and who-
ever studies himself really attentively will
find in himself, yes, even in his judgment,
this gyration and discord. I have nothing
to say about myself absolutely, simply, and
solidly, without confusion and without
mixture, or in one word (1957, II, p. 242).

If Montaigne cannot make definite statements about himself—the subject he presumably
knows best—what can be said of his knowledge
of more distant subjects? It is provisional, subject to change, and always dependent upon the
"posture" of the knower. Contemporary theorists
would say that we construct knowledge, actively
shaping it through the use of language and other
symbol systems. We do not mirror some fixed
and permanent external reality (Rorty, 1979).

Montaigne's "essay" was then a formless form, open enough to allow for the explorations of a reality which was fundamentally unstable. The reader of the essay, like the participant in a good conversation, did not seek to carry away precepts or conclusions. Montaigne claimed that he was more concerned with the "manner" of speaking than the "matter," the "form" as much as the "substance"—"In the same way I seek the company of some famous mind not so that he might teach me, but that I might know him" (1580, 1958, p. 293). The manner of the seeking, the wondering was more important than the truthfulness of that which is found—because any truth was provisional, sure to be undone or revised by subsequent inquiries. The pedant, on the other hand, was like a bird who carried grain at the tip of its beak, not tasting it, and passing it on to baby birds. The pedants "pillaged" the ancients, but failed to taste; they picked up precepts, but ignored the manner of inquiry.

The essay was for Montaigne a "common ground," on which he could explore issues that could not be confined to a specialty, ones common to all humans: among topics were smells, the custom of wearing clothes, the pain of kidney

stones, the affection of fathers for children, conversation, friendship, and sneezing (its relation-
ship to belching). He can occupy this common
ground because his writing is grounded in his
own experience:

> I would rather understand myself well
> by self-study than by reading Cicero. In
> the experience that I have with myself I
> have enough to make me wise, if I am a
> good scholar (1958, p. 354).

Despite the hundreds of references to classical literature in his essays, the most basic
source of knowledge, fluctuating and unstable as
it might be, is rigorous self-study. The essay, as
Montaigne defined it and practiced it, is irreduc-
ibly personal.

E. B. White, one of Montaigne's heirs, strikes
almost exactly the same note in the introduction
to his collected essays:

> The essayist is a self-liberated man,
> sustained by the childish belief that ev-
> erything he thinks about, everything that
> happens to him, is of general interest. He is
> a fellow who thoroughly enjoys his work,
> just as people who take bird walks enjoy
> theirs. Each new excursion, each new

"attempt" differs from the last and takes him to new country. This delights him. Only a person who is congenitally self-centered has the effrontery and stamina to write essays (1977, p. vii).

While the classical argument is pictures as an edifice (a structure with supports) or a battleground (in which positions are staked out and defended), the essay is more often pictured as a journey. But it is not, in Montaigne's words, a "solemn march"—it is more an amble or, as White claims, the kind of walk a bird-watcher might take. Clifford Geertz (1983) extends this metaphor:

For making detours and going by sideroads, nothing is more convenient than the essay form. One can take off in almost any direction, certain that if the thing does not work out one can turn back and start over in some other at moderate cost.... Wanderings into yet smaller side-roads and wider detours does little harm, for progress is not expected to be relentlessly forward, but winding and improvisational, coming out where it comes out. And when there is nothing more to say on the subject at the moment, or perhaps altogether, the matter can simply be dropped. "Works are not finished," as Valery said, "they are abandoned" (1983, p. 6).

What a far cry from the advice we give students!

Now this kind of exploration has, in recent years, gained a place in composition pedagogy as a *pre-writing* strategy. In many classes students are encouraged to free-write and produce what Linda Flower (1979) has called "writer-based prose" which must then be transformed into more tightly structured "reader-based prose." In other words, these meanderings and digressions, while they are often necessary to help the writer discover what he or she wants to say, need to be stripped from the writing that the reader eventually gets. The reader that Flower posits is clearly not one who is along for the ride.

In his 1985 Braddock Award essay, Peter Elbow argues that distinctions such as those which contrast the conversation-like exploration that occurs in free-writing with finished, well-crafted expository prose may be missing the features of the essay that actually appeal to us. In effect, Elbow is attempting to rescue free-writing from its designation as a pre-writing technique.

He begins by asking us to re-examine what we mean by structure in exposition. The predominant view of structure is schematic or visual—it can be represented in diagram or outline or in some form of visual display. The essay is seen as an architectural whole with beams, and of course, supports. Elbow claims that this schematic, visual view is flawed, in part because we experience a text through time and not as a timeless whole.

As readers, we *experience* structure as movement through the text; we are propelled from paragraph to paragraph or we come to a standstill, moving on only out of a sense of duty. We can be carried along in an essay that cannot be clearly diagrammed (Montaigne is a good example), and we can balk at a structured essay that builds no momentum. Writers build this momentum not by withholding or transforming the mental processes of exploration but by revealing them and allowing the reader to participate in them. "It's as though the writer's mental activity is somehow there in the words on the page—as though the silent words are somehow alive with her meaning" (Elbow, 1985, p. 299). This, one suspects, is the surprising realization that Montaigne's readers made 400 years ago.

If participation in the mental activity of the writer compels us to read on, it is clear that the thesis-control paper may work against this participation because the form is so front-loaded. Readers are given too much, too early. The writer builds no sense of anticipation because the conclusion is offered at the very beginning. Elbow writes:

> Unless there is a felt question—a tension, a palpable itch—the time remains unbound. The most common reason why weak essays don't hang together is that the writing is all statement, all consonance, all answer: the reader is not made to experience any cognitive dissonance to serve as a "net" or "set" to catch all these statements or answers. Without an itch or a sense of a felt problem, nothing holds the reader's experience together—however well the text itself might summarize the parts (p. 296).

It is counterproductive, according to this argument, to encourage students to begin essays with answers to questions that have not yet been raised in the reader's mind.

This view also has advantages for the writer. It's useful to ask the basic question —why write? What in the act of writing can give the writer pleasure? To be sure we can name external rewards—promotion, publication, graduation. But if writing is to be more than a duty—like going to the dental hygienist—we need to speculate on the pleasure that writers find in the act of writing itself.

Fiction writers consistently claim that they are motivated by moving into the unknown. Toni Morrison writes:

> I write out of ignorance. I write about the things I don't have any resolutions for, and when I'm finished, I think I know a little bit more about it. I don't write out of what I know. It's what I don't know that stimulates me (quoted in Murray, 1989, p. 174).

Writers also describe a state of receptivity, in which they personify the material they're writing about. Donald Murray speaks of "the informing line," one which can indicate the direction or focus of an entire piece of writing. He claims that the evolving text will tell him what to write. Eudora Welty urges writers to "let the story arise of itself. Let it speak for itself.

Let it reveal itself as it goes along" (quoted in Murray, 1989, p. 176).

Clearly, the writer is more than a "medium" for writing to somehow pass through; the writer's mind is active even as the story seems to arise of its own accord. But the sensation of a story seeming to take on a life of its own is so pervasive in writer's accounts, that it must have some psychological validity. If the resolutions to stories had to be determined ahead of time; if the characters were fully formed in the writer's mind; if writing became merely an act of transcription, of carrying out detailed plans, its appeal would vanish. Without the lure of uncertainty and surprise, writing would be drudgery. If beginning writers never have this experience of the writing taking over—the emerging language outpacing the original intention, the digression becoming a central part of the writing—they will never understand what it is that motivates writers. And the essay must be open enough for this movement into the unknown.

Now it is time to back up. Students need to learn how to deal with situations where they are confronting potentially hostile or at least skeptical readers—where they must stake out a position and defend it. And there are situations where students will meet the impatient reader who is interested in the results of inquiry rather than the journey the writer has taken. But there is a more patient and companionable reader that likes the open road and the loose itinerary. The problem is one of balance. William Zeigler (1985) writes:

> ...concentration on the expository essay has reached the point of severely diminished returns. It continually demands that the writer prove a thesis, even while slighting the exploration that would provide the substance of the proof; it asks the writer to make bricks without straw.... If we genuinely wish to promote freedom of thought, to balance demonstration with the inquiry which sustains it, then we must establish the art of exploration as an equally acceptable and worthy pursuit (p. 459).

The question remains—how? One of the clear advantages of the thesis-control paper is the fact that the students can be taught to master the form. Simply urging students to explore ideas in open-ended essays is more likely to create panic and frustration than a feeling of self-liberation. One solution, it seems to me, is not to abandon

the idea of structure altogether, but to help students attempt structures that are more "open"
than the thesis-control paper, ones which allow
for movement toward conclusion and resolution.

Invitations
to the Essay

My doctoral advisor once said that his original ideas were those for which he had forgotten the source. The same can be said for most writing assignments. Like the jokes we tell, most assignments have been around in one form or another for a long time. The following assignments were used in beginning college writing courses at the University of New Hampshire. They are not presented as personal inventions or as a sequence to be used, but as attempts to reclaim the essay.

Reading Narratives

Students bring to their reading two myths that inhibit their ability to deal with difficult texts. The first is the myth of instant comprehension—texts give up their meaning without a fight. School systems perpetuate this myth through timed reading achievement tests which put a premium on speed so that students naturally learn to distrust their own abilities when they meet something that is, on first reading, puzzling. The second misconception might be called the myth of complete comprehension—those texts that do give up their meanings do so completely and unambiguously. Meanings are determinate, fixed for all time. And a good reading leads to this fixed meaning. Ambiguity is only a virtue for English teachers who love to make the simple difficult and the clear unclear.

The myths clearly work to the student's disadvantage when reading difficult texts, especially modern poetry. The student who expects comprehension to be instant and unambiguous is not likely to sustain what John Dewey called an "attitude of suspended conclusion" when reading poetry. To help foster this attitude in one of my college English courses, I began asking students to compose reading narratives. I would hand out a Xeroxed copy of a poem and ask them to mark it up as they read: they were to mark words or expressions that struck them, that confused them; they were to look for shifts in the poem and for words or phrases which gained significance on a second or third reading. For each reading of the poem, I asked them to mark it with a different writing tool so that there would be a clear set of "tracks" which could be used in writing the narrative.

In asking students to highlight significant words or phrases, I am working against the belief that all words are created equal and must be attended to equally. Without selective attention there is no field, no ground. As Bartholomae and Anthony Petrosky note (1986), interpretation begins with the act of selective remembering (and, of course, selective forgetting). The student begins to discriminate, to assign significance—"this caught my attention (and this did not)."

When students determined that their reading of the poem was completed, they were asked to write a short (about 150-300 word) narrative describing what happened to them when they read the poem. The key word here is "describe"—the paper was not to be an argument or a full interpretation that would compete with other interpretations written in the class. My feeling was that the competitive atmosphere of many critical analysis classes causes students to mask certain basic difficulties. As Elbow points out in *Writing without Teachers* (1973), descriptive statements cannot be debated in the same way that interpretations can. If I claim to be puzzled by a particular shift from one stanza to the next, another reader cannot deny my puzzlement, even though he or she may not have had the same difficulty.

By asking students to write narratives, I was also trying to match the form of writing to the time-bound experience of reading. We do not experience texts as the timeless wholes so dear to the hearts of the New Critics—we move through them, word by word, stanza by stanza. Even in the more traditional critical analysis paper, we are drawing on accumulated *narrative* experiences with the poem.

I will quote excerpts from two of the students' narratives to give an idea of how these narrative experiences were used. In the poem "Tornado" (Hedin, 1982), there are two sets of images that to many students had no direct connection: the images of the tornado and images "of the bulls my father slaughtered every August/ How he would pull out of the rank sea/ A pair of collapsed lungs, stomach,/ Eight bushels of

gleaming rope he called intestines." One student
worked at reconciling these images as follows:

> The first time through the poem it
> seemed to make no coherent sense except
> the lines of the first stanza reminded me of
> the tornadoes I'd seen and lived through
> in Nebraska. During the second reading I
> realized that the rest of the poem seemed
> disjointed from any experience I ever had
> with tornadoes. The third time through
> was no more enlightening about what the
> second and third stanzas were trying to
> put across to the reader. My fourth time
> through was when it all came to light af-
> ter just a little thinking and reflection; it
> dawned on me that he is comparing his fa-
> ther and the slaughter of the bulls to the
> tornado and its devastating properties of
> pulling things right out of the ground.

As a teacher reading this account, I felt priv-
ileged to get inside the mind of this student, to
watch the movement from an undefined and general sense of something not making sense, to a
more specific sense of the problem, to a possible
resolution of the problem.

Not all narratives lead directly from a sense
of difficulty to a sense of resolution. In one re-

sponse to Theodore Roethke's "Moss Gathering" (1961) a student worked his way through difficulties in the poem only to discover a new problem on the third reading. It suddenly occurred to him that there is a conflict between his own personal image of moss gathering and the language Roethke uses to describe it: "afterwards I always felt mean.../ By pulling off flesh from a living planet;/ As if I committed, against the whole scheme of life, a desecration."

> This is really far-fetched, but I get the feeling of impending doom as I read this. "Cemetery," "Old fashioned," "hollow," "underside," "old," "natural order of things," "pulling off the flesh," "desecration," and "went out," all bring to mind scenes of death/destruction. Lord, I don't get it. He's talking about moss-gathering. Why should he be interested in why/how things die? I don't see the connection. All the transitions are clear now so long as I don't hang up on the "evil" words.

The student's concluding statement was, "What the hell is going on?" It took this student three readings to come to a "problem" which, while unresolved, goes a long way toward explaining the discomfort we feel in reading Roethke's poem. We are asked to experience this act of lifting the moss from the soil, not as a pleasurable act, but as one of violence, a desecration for which, as the student senses, we may be punished. Hence the feeling of impending doom. Paradoxically, the writer's deepest penetration into the poem comes when he's convinced he doesn't know "what the hell is going on."

These readings narratives can be used in different ways:

• They can be shared in small groups and can be used to initiate a discussion of a poem. Students might also write a second narrative after the discussion since hearing the responses of other students may alert them to more in the poem.

• The student can accumulate a number of reading narratives and can write what I have called elsewhere (Newkirk, 1984) a "reading profile." In this paper the writer examines the individual narratives and identifies general strategies he or she uses when reading poetry.

Reflective Paper

The reflective paper that I have also used is built on the same premises as the reading narratives—that a form should allow space for the writer to formulate a problem, and the writing itself can be used to resolve the problem. In this way, the writer creates what Elbow (1985) calls an "anticipatory frame," an "itch" to be scratched. The reader also has the opportunity to follow the mental processes of the writer as the tension is resolved.

For the reflective paper I ask students to identify an experience that "caused them to think." It could be one that forced them to think in a different way about themselves or someone close to them. It could be a situation that caused them to question their own system of values. As preparatory reading I use a paper written by one of Donald Murray's students, Dale Paul (1985). The paper, included in Coles and Vopat's *What Makes Writing Good?*, is entitled, "Without Child," and begins with a triggering incident:

> The toy shop was so tiny that I had to be careful not to step on children playing with the sturdy samples. Searching for a wooden train to send to my nephew, squeezing

between a hobby horse and a grandmother,
I found myself face to face with an infant
in a backpack. Brown eyes peeped out of
an absurd white ruffled bonnet and she
was crowing with delight at the commo-
tion. Smiling back at her, I was horrified to
find my eyes full of tears. Where had they
come from? (p. 105)

The essay is an attempt to answer that question—where had they come from? Paul recounts
her initial reaction to the news that she would
not be able to have a child, and her attempts to
deal rationally and reasonably with that news.
She concludes her essay by rejecting this reason-
ableness:

I will not have a child of my own, will
never experience pregnancy, will never
give birth. That is a loss which needs to
be mourned. I don't need to examine the
options rationally. I need to feel angry and
sad and grieve. The women in my generation have not yet learned to mourn.

Packing away the Christmas decorations
this year, I wondered what will become of
them when my husband and I die. We have
been collectors, makers of tradition. Of
what use is tradition if there is no generation to inherit it? (p.106)

"Without Child" is a moving piece of writing—moving, in part, because we move *with* the writer from an initial sense of uncomprehending sadness, through unsuccessful attempts to deal with the problem "reasonably," to the painful resolution of the last two paragraphs.

Several students adapted this structure when they wrote their own papers. One, Kathy Chang, wrote about living in her almost unbearably crowded apartment above a lei shop in Honolulu's Chinatown. Her parents paid no rent for the apartment, staying there at the pleasure of the owners, whom Kathy refers to as "downstairs":

> To this day we must abide by the rules of "downstairs." I remember when I was only six-years-old and came home from school. I had to say hello to everyone downstairs every day; I had to say hello to those mean faces who meant me harm.... (once in our apartment) I wanted to yell my frustrations because the noise I made might arouse customers' curiosity or just irritate "downstairs." I stared at the clock, it said three o'clock. Time for Checkers and Pogo. So I turned on the television and sat back, trying to wipe from my memory

the faces I just saw. My mother came up to me and told me I had to turn the TV off or watch with no sound and reminded me not to make any noises or fight with my little brother. She feared that if "downstairs" passed the door and heard the TV or us, then they would think that we were just lazy bums with nothing else better to do and might just tell us off on the spot.

Kathy uses the first part of the paper to establish the corrosive effects of dependency on "downstairs." But the breakpoint comes one sweltering night when she is trying to do her homework in the crowded dining room:

The back door was locked shut because the alley cats would come in if it were open. The two heavy windows in the front of the house were as wide open as they could be but only the unpleasant stuffiness could be felt throughout the household.... The old floor and table creaked as I rested myself into the chair. I glanced at the wall with the chipped paint and saw a parade of ants marching single file in both directions ready to attack a piece of our dinner that someone had left and didn't bother to pick up. "This couldn't be happening to me," I pleaded silently to God.

Her mother comes in to tell her she will have to finish her homework before her uncle (who sleeps in the living room) comes home. Then Kathy explodes, "Why can't we just move out already, things are so damn inconvenient. I'm sick and tired of living like this. Things should get better."

Her mother lowers her voice and reminds Kathy that "downstairs" has threatened to kick them out again, and would surely do it if they heard an argument. At this point the essay turns back on itself. She begins to see that her own parents have also suffered; she realizes that they can not yet move out of the apartment:

> After the lecture from my mother I was speechless and walked to my room in silence. As I lay in the dark I began to reflect on the times I had blown up and blamed my parents for the house that we lived in. Blaming them, saying it was their fault when it wasn't.

Kathy at this point realizes that she is not alone in feeling the pressure from "downstairs," that her mother, too, has to endure the suspicion and the economic insecurity of taking charity. While her conclusion is not startling, it is one that first generation immigrants have had to live with for hundreds of years—things will get better, our time will come, but until it does we need to endure alley cats, ants marching on the wall, and an uncle sleeping in the living room.

It is interesting to speculate about how these two essays would have been different if the authors' conclusions had been stated early on as thesis statements. As they now stand, the conclusions have power not because they are startling truths, but because of the speculation and the examination of experience that went into them. They are *earned* insights; and we respect them, are moved by them, because we have had access to the process of their formulation. Had Paul's conclusion been stated as a thesis statement early on in her essay—something like "women of my generation have been brought up to expect everything and are unprepared...."—I suspect we would have found it ineffective. We wouldn't be prepared for a generalization of that magnitude—although we are ready for it at the end of the essay. We accept at the end of her essay what we probably would have balked at in the beginning.

Parallel Narratives

When we talk about books we often cycle between recounting passages in the book, sharing reactions, and relating incidents or ideas in the book to our own experiences. Some books and essays "read us," illuminating our own lives as we go. When I recently reread E. B. White's "Once More to the Lake," I was struck by the way he sees generations repeating each other. I thought of a photograph taken when I was five at the Ohio farm of one of my uncles. I am sitting on an old tractor with a wide "say cheese" smile, holding on tightly to the steering wheel. When I showed the picture to my son, he was convinced it was of him, and he even claimed to remember when it was taken. He had become me, and I had become my father, and my father was now an old man.

White's essay triggered this memory, and it allowed me to think about this picture in a new way. Borrowing from Richard Hugo's concept of a "triggering subject" (1979), my colleague Donna Qualley has used the term "triggering text" in her composition classes. The text acts as a memory probe; we locate an experience that had been buried or that seemed insignificant. And, simul-

sly, the reading provides an interpretive
-White's reference to "the chill of death"
nd of the essay made me aware that the
sturbed me because I had become what
father was, and would become what he is.

In a number of composition classes we ask
students to react to texts that trigger memories
and reflections on their own lives. The writing
students then balance commentary on the essay
or book with personal recollection and reflection
(Chiseri-Strater, 1988). To illustrate the parallel
narrative that can result, I will reproduce the
opening to a paper by sophomore Danya Linehan
in which she develops her own connections to
"Once More to the Lake." This paper is a second
draft, written after in-class discussion of the essay and a conference with her teacher:

Magical Childhood Experiences

As I read "Once More to the Lake," I first
thought E. B. White was lucky to venture
back to a magical childhood place and find
it almost unchanged. The lake was still
not a "wild lake" he said, and the bed-
room had the same timber smell and va-
cationers still ate dinner at the farmhouse.
White was struck however with the pas-

sage of time and his lost youth. The road was barren, Coca-cola had replaced Moxie, outboard motors now broke the silence and his "groin felt the chill of death" as he watched his son yank up a wet suit after a thunderstorm. White's journey back to the lake brought up mixed emotions.

The first childhood memory I tried to re-live was a disaster. A few years ago I went back to Animal Forest in Maine. It used to be a fantasy land for me where llamas, sheep, and goats roamed free. They romped and played with humans. I still have the scar near my belly button where an adolescent goat butted me.

But as I approached the park on my return visit, I noticed, as White did, that the sound was not right. White heard the "unfamiliar nervous sound of outboard motors," and I heard the loud scraping of machinery, carnival music, and screaming kids. "Languidly and with no thought of going in," I stood teary-eyed in the tar-covered entrance. In place of my Animal Forest, I found a cheap amusement park filled with rides and popcorn stands. All that remained of my memory was a handful of well-fed goats in a corner pen.

I don't feel old enough to experience the "chill of death" as White did. But the scene at the Animal Forest gave me a brutal shove into adulthood. This was no longer my Animal Forest and it never would be again; this park belonged to the children of the eighties. As I returned to my car, I shivered to think there was no turning back.

This paper would probably be unacceptable in a traditional literary analysis class—too much Danya and too little White. The structure is associational rather than hierarchical; the paper is empathetic rather than strictly analytical. It lacks "rigor."

But questions about intellectual standards, about more advanced and less advanced ways of thinking, are rarely as clear-cut as we make them out to be. In *The Unbearable Lightness of Being*, Milan Kundera writes:

> The very beginning of Genesis tells us that God created man in order to give him dominion over fish and fowl and all creatures. Of course, Genesis was written by a man, not a horse. There is no certainty that God actually did grant man dominion over other creatures. What seems more likely, in

fact, is that man invented God to sanctify
the dominion he had usurped for himself
over the cow and horse (1985, p. 286).

Universities and schools similarly subscribe
to hierarchies of knowing with some kinds of
thinking—usually the theoretical, analytical,
distanced, abstract, and logical—considered to
be higher level. By contract, those cognitive processes that are empathetic, affective, personal,
situated, narrative, and strongly dependent on
memory, are thought to be at a lower level (see,
for example, Bloom *et al*, 1959). There is a pre-
dilection for the metaphor of "height" in these
descriptions, as if what was being evaluated was
no more controversial or value-laden than deter-
mining if redwoods were taller than maples.

Feminists like Gilligan (1982) and Belenky
et al (1986) have argued that these schemes are
not innocent of ideology; rather they reflect the
values of the male dominated academic environ-
ments in which they were developed. Traditional
models of academic achievement discriminate
against women who may favor a more personal,
empathetic, "connected" style of engagement
over one that is distancing and argumentative.

Indeed, it may be "written" that analysis and abstraction are the ends of education, the highest forms of thinking—but who is doing the writing? Or, as we said on the playground, "Says who?"

Kyle thought he was a topic sentence but after ten years of marriage he realized he was just a supporting detail.

"I'm not going to talk about it"

A few years ago I asked students to respond to an essay by Gloria Steinem in which she discusses premarital sex. Several students dutifully summarized her points, but the essay set at least one student to thinking:

> I may be considered an old fart by guys with no brains but I disagree with Steinem and her statement that sex before marriage was designed to oppress women. I guess it's just my strong Christian background. Steinem is absolutely correct, I feel, when she says that sexual intercourse can be an intimate form of communication. However it is my belief that communication this intimate should be kept for marriage. I'm

not sure how I would feel if the unmarried couples are honestly and truly in love. I know what I'm supposed to think according to the Bible. I'm supposed to think no way until marriage but in my mind I lean toward Steinem's belief in this case. Then however, we get into the discussion of what is true love. I'm not going to talk about it (quoted in Newkirk, 1983, p.9).

This is the kind of writing my high school books warned about, a straying from the path. The writer begins by disagreeing with Steinem, and ends by leaning toward her belief. He is more confused at the end of the essay than he was at the beginning. But I prefer this response over the others that tied things together; for his opens up a conversation, rather than closing things down. There are open spaces in his essay that we can talk about.

As a teacher of writing, of essays, I look for these open spaces, where the writer hints at a territory into which he or she can move. Often the hint is a loaded line ("It's awful to be told you have potential"), the exposed tip of a major perception. It may be a clause like "but in my mind I lean to…." when a writer pushes beyond an accepted view. It may be only an intuition that an impersonal paper on eating disorders has its roots in significant experiences that need to be explored. Often it is a place where the writer seems to lose control, where the writing becomes disjointed, where it strays. I find this type of "bad writing" far more satisfying than the more contained writing that wins American Legion writing contests, that has the seamless confident tone of the graduation speech.

At the beginning of the *Phaedrus*, Socrates meets young Phaedrus and asks him, "Where have you come from, my dear Phaedrus, and where are you going?" It is, I believe, more than just a casual question—it is *the* question that we need to ask students. If writing is to be a "unique mode of thinking," we should ask how writing can foster and track movement of the mind. It is time to reclaim the essay from the writing textbooks where it has been immobilized.

References

Baker, Sheridan, and Yarber, Robert. *The Practical Stylist With Readings*, Sixth Edition. New York: Harper and Row, 1986.

Bartholomae, David. "Writing assignments: Where writing begins." In Patricia Strock, (Ed.), *FORUM: Essays on Theory and Practice in the Teaching of Writing*. Upper Montclair, New Jersey: Boynton / Cook, 1983.

Bartholomae, David, and Petrosky, Anthony. *Facts, Artifacts, and Counterfacts*. Upper Montclair, New Jersey: Boynton / Cook, 1983.

Bean-Thompson, Janet. "Curveballs, contradictions, and confusions: An approach to critical writing." In *Classroom Practices in the Teaching of English 1989: Writing and Literature*, in press.

Belenky, Mary, *et al. Women's Ways of Knowing: The Development of Self, Voice and Mind.* New York: Basic Books, 1986.

Bloom, Benjamin, (Ed.). *Taxonomy of Educational Objectives: The Classification of Goals by Committee of College and University Examiners.* New York: Longman, Green, 1959.

Chiseri-Strater, Elizabeth. "Welcome to my world too: Connecting reading and writing," *English Record, 39*, (2), 1988, pp. 20-24.

Covino, William. *The Art of Wondering: A Revisionist Return to the History of Rhetoric.* Portsmouth, New Hampshire: Boynton / Cook, 1988.

Durst, Russel. "The development of analytic writing." In Arthur Applebee, (Ed.), *Contexts for Learning to Write: Studies of Secondary School Instruction.* Norwood, New Jersey: ABLEX, 1984, pp.79-102.

Elbow, Peter. "The shifting relationships between speech and writing," *College Composition and Communication*, 35 (3), October 1985, pp. 283-303.

Elbow, Peter. *Writing without Teachers*. New York: Oxford University Press, 1973.

Emig, Janet. "From The Composing Processes of Twelfth Graders (chapters 4, 6, and 7)." In Janet Emig, (Ed.) *The Web of Meaning: Essays on Writing, Teaching, Learning, and Thinking*. Upper Montclair, New Jersey: Boynton / Cook, 1971, 1983, pp. 65-96.

Emig, Janet. "Writing as a mode of learning." In Janet Emig (Ed.), *The Web of Meaning: Essays on Writing, Teaching, Learning, and Thinking*. Upper Montclair, New Jersey: Boynton / Cook, 1977, 1983, pp. 122-131.

Flower, Linda. "Writer-based prose: A cognitive basis for problems in writing," College English, 41, (3), 1979, pp. 19-37.

Geertz, Clifford. *Local Knowledge: Further Essays in Interpretive Anthropology*. New York: Basic Books, 1983.

Gilligan, Carol. *In a Different Voice: Psychological Theory and Women's Development*. Cambridge, Massachusetts: Harvard University Press, 1982.

Goody, Jack. *Literacy in Traditional Societies*. Cambridge, England: Cambridge University Press, 1968.

—. *The Domestication of the Savage Mind.* Cambridge, England: Cambridge University Press, 1977.

Hedin, Robert. "Tornado," *Poetry*, 140, 1982, p. 28.

Hoagland, Edward. "What I think, what I am." In William Smart, (Ed.), *Eight Modern Essayists*, Fourth Edition. New York: St. Martins, 1985.

Hugo, Richard. *The Triggering Town.* New York: Norton, 1979.

Kundera, Milan. *The Unbearable Lightness of Being.* New York: Harper and Row, 1985.

Laib, Nevin. "Territoriality in rhetoric," *College English, 47* (6), 1985, pp. 579-593.

Marshall, James. "Classroom discourse and literary response." In Ben Nelms, (Ed.), *Readers, Texts, and Contexts: Literature in the Classroom.* Urbana, Illinois: National Council of Teachers of English, 1988, pp. 45-58.

Montaigne, Michel de. *The Complete Works of Montaigne.* Donald Frame, trans., Stanford: Stanford University Press, 1957.

Montaigne, Michel de. *Essays*. John Florio, trans., New York: Pocket Books, 1580, 1959.

Montaigne, Michel de. *Essays*. J. M. Cohen, trans., Harmondsworth, England: Penguin Books, 1580, 1958.

Murray, Donald. *Expecting the Unexpected: Teaching Myself – and Others – to Read and Write*. Portsmouth, New Hampshire: Boynton / Cook-Heinemann, 1989.

Newkirk, Thomas. "Looking for trouble: A way to unmask our readings," *College English, 46* (8), 1984, pp. 756-766.

Newkirk, Thomas. "Why bother with William Perry," *English Record, 34* (3), 1983, pp. 9-11.

Ong, Walter. *Interfaces of the Word*. Ithaca, New York: Cornell University Press, 1977.

Paul, Dale. "Without child." In William E. Coles, Jr. and James Vopat, *What Makes Writing Good: A Multiperspective*. Lexington, Massachusetts: D.C. Heath, 1985, pp. 105-106.

Payne, Lucile. *The Lively Art of Writing*. Chicago: Follett, 1965.

Plato. *The Phaedrus*. Walter Hamilton, trans., Harmondsworth, England; Penguin Books, 1973.

Roethke, Theodore. "Moss gathering." In *Words for the Wind: The Collected Verse of Theodore Roethke*. Bloomington, Indiana: Indiana University Press, 1971.

Rorty, Richard. *Philosophy and the Mirror of Nature*. Princeton: Princeton University Press, 1979.

Spellmeyer, Kurt. "A common ground : The essay in the academy," *College English, 51* (3), 1989, pp. 262-276.

Street, Brian. *Literacy in Theory and Practice*. Cambridge, England: Cambridge University Press, 1984.

Warriner, John, Whitten, Mary, and Griffith, Francis. *English Grammar and Composition*. New York: Harcourt, Brace, and World, 1965.

Watson, James. *The Double Helix*. New York: New American Library, 1969.

White, E.B. *Essays of E.B. White*. New York: Harper and Row, 1977.

Zeigler, William. "The exploratory essay: En-franchising the spirit of inquiry in college composition," *College English, 47* (5), 1985, pp. 454-466.

Thomas Newkirk is a Professor of English at the University of New Hampshire where he has directed the Freshman English Program and where he founded and directs the New Hampshire Literacy Institutes. He has written extensively on literacy learning at all grade levels, winning the 2000 David Russell Award for his book, *The Performance of Self in Student Writing.* His most recent book is *Misreading Masculinity: Boys, Literacy, and Popular Culture* (Heinemann).

The Practical Guide for Bringing Life to School Essays

If you agree with Thomas Newkirk, you will want to read this practical companion guide written by Teacher/Author Gretchen Bernabei. These classroom-tested lessons will show you many ways for bringing life to school essays.

Available with other titles from your local DWP book rep or at www.discoverwriting.com

Discover Writing Press